Advance praise for
Pray for Today

"*Pray for Today* does not proselytize. It's not unlike sitting down to tea, enjoying a nice, quiet chat with a friend and when it's time to leave, discovering that you've been introduced to a completely new concept about prayer and how it can become an integral part of your life. In *Pray for Today*, Barb Rogers shares that wisdom in such a way that no matter what religion or belief you embrace, even if none at all, you will be inspired to give prayer a try. You have nothing to lose and a far more fulfilled life to gain."
—Chassie West, author of the
Leigh Ann Warren Mysteries

"You'll find *Pray for Today* especially useful if you've wanted to pray and did not quite know how, or if your prayer life has grown stagnant."
—Philip Goldberg, author of *Roadsigns: Navigating Your
Path to Spiritual Happiness* and *Making Peace with God*

"Inspirational and essential. The perfect book to read for a spiritual pick-me-up. I love Barb Rogers's easy style and common sense."
—Elizabeth Engstrom, author of *Black Leather*

"Beautiful! A simple, inspiring guide to living a life of peace and love through prayer and surrender."
—Kathy Cordova, author of *Let Go, Let Miracles Happen*

Pray for Today

just
try
this

Pray for Today

Barb Rogers

Red Wheel
Boston, MA / York Beach, ME

First published in 2005 by
Red Wheel/Weiser, LLC
York Beach, ME
With offices at:
368 Congress Street
Boston, MA 02210
www.redwheelweiser.com

LIBRARY OF CONGRESS CATALOGING-IN-PUBLICATION DATA
Rogers, Barb.
  Pray for today / Barb Rogers.
      p. cm.
  ISBN 1-59003-074-5
  1. Prayer—Christianity. I. Title.
  BV210.3.R64 2004
  248.3'2—dc22
                              2004016447
Typeset in MrsEaves and Dalliance by Kathleen Wilson Fivel
Printed in Canada
TCP
12 11 10 09 08 07 06 05
  8 7 6 5 4 3 2 1

In loving memory of Helen Wright, my friend,
my teacher, who was truly an earthbound angel.
And to her family, the Highlands.
Thank you for including me in your family.
You'll never know the difference it made in my life.

Contents

Introduction

Some people say we are deluding ourselves by believing in God to make our lives seem more tolerable. They suggest that prayer is nothing more than an exercise in frustration. There is no real point to our existence, they say, and our lives end at the grave. I was one of those people.

At thirty-five, I thought I had nothing left to live for. I'd been stripped down to nothing. I'd outlived my children, what family I had left wanted nothing to do with me, even friends I thought were in worse shape had deserted me. All my possessions were gone, and I had no idea who or what I was—except a mess. I lived in half of a garage; didn't own a television, radio, or even a fan; walked to work most of the time; had to count how many sodas a week I could afford to buy; and lived on soup and crackers that I had to share with my dog so we might both survive.

A funny thing happened on my way to suicide. I discovered a flicker of hope, a small flame of life living deep within my heart. If I could just find a way to live for one more day, maybe my life wouldn't be totally worthless.

I wanted to live, but I didn't want to live this way. I believe God took care of me even before I was able, or willing, to ask him for help. Granted, my life was not good, but he made me see that I was still alive, and where there is life, there is hope. All it has to be is a tiny flicker, a pinpoint of light, a small wondering.

Through messages given me by others who had been down a similar path, my hope grew. I wondered, I watched, I listened. Prayer was the one thing they all had in common. They said I didn't even have to truly believe; I just had to find the willingness to try it. I became desperate enough to try, to use their spiritual exercises to get started. In my desperation, I cried out for help with one problem each day. It worked!

With each baby step I took, I got stronger, my spiritual muscle grew. Each time I came to prayer and the solution was made clear to me, I was amazed. The answers were not always easy, and I had to do things I didn't want to do to take care of problems, but the results were worth it.

At thirty-seven, I surrendered my life to the God of my understanding, gave him all that I was on a daily basis. My life was waiting for me, the life God wanted me to live. It was no longer a worthless existence, nor had it ever really been worthless. Everything that had gone before, everything that brought me to my knees, was shaping me for what was to come.

God has given me more than I ever dared to dream. All I had to do was open myself up to the possibilities and do the work required.

1 *Is Anyone Out There?*

*G*od, that elusive being, with many faces and names, is not that hard to find. He's not the one who has been lost.

"Do you believe? Do you *really* believe?" I've heard ministers yell that out to their audience. Perhaps what they need to ask is, "Do you wonder?"

If life flows like a river, with each of us in our own canoe, and you are paddling upstream as hard as you can and getting nowhere, or your canoe is swamped and sinking, you might wonder what it would be like to turn it around. Well, the choice is yours—and wondering is the first tug in the other direction. It might be a struggle, but it can be done.

Now that you've begun to question, to wonder if there might be a better way, it's time to consider faith. Faith is a sense of knowing without understanding. When you think about it, we practice faith every day without even realizing it. When we walk into a room and flip the light switch, we have faith that the bulb will light up. There is no need to understand the mechanics of electricity for the light to enhance our life. What if spirituality could be that simple? And what if the light switch is prayer?

One of the most potent prayers ever uttered is, "God, help me!" It doesn't matter whether you're standing at the altar of a cathedral, in your house, on a beach, or in your canoe. If you have spoken those heartfelt words, you've opened the lines of communication. You've opened your heart to the possibility that there is something out there greater than yourself. You've acknowledged that you need guidance.

I've heard many people tell stories about having a spiritual awakening. They speak of a light shining through their window in the darkness, of seeing angels, of hearing a voice, but that was not my experience. My spiritual awakening was more of a feeling, a feeling I'd never experienced before. It was as if someone had engulfed me in a warm embrace, and I just knew everything would be okay—no matter what happened, it would be okay. I knew I was not alone and would never have to be again—as long as I kept that connection.

If the best you can do on a daily basis is say those three words, "God, help me," that's enough. Those three words are a kind of prayer, and you will be amazed at the difference it can make in your life. You might not be in control of many things in your life, but you are in control of the light switch, of staying connected through prayer to a God of your choosing.

With practice and prayer, wonder turns to faith. Some might take their newfound faith to a church, to pray in groups; others will hold a personal relationship with God in the privacy of their home. It doesn't matter how eloquently we pray or where we pray; what matters is the feeling behind the words.

As a matter of course, faith will be put into action. Prayer is the same as deed. If we give with one hand and take with the other, what good is our giving? If we pray and ask for help and then do the opposite of what we know is right, it's the same problem. What is the point of asking our guide for direction if we are going to go our own way anyway? When we pray, we are asking for direction and guidance, not an opinion. We can get opinions from other people who probably don't know much more about life than we do. After all, how can another person, even one who knows us well, guide us when they can see no farther down the road than we can?

If there is a plan, and if we are part of that plan, then I don't believe any human can show us the way to faith. They might share with us their own experience—how they were brought to prayer, how they made the connection, had a spiritual awakening—but we are all unique, with different life experiences, with our own beliefs. We are all seeking the same thing, but we will each get there in our own way, when the time is right for us. It takes what it takes—every life experience good and bad, other people who pass through our lives, all the highs and lows—until in our need for relief, we utter that very potent prayer, "God, help me!"

2 | Can You Hear Me, God?

*A*s a child, I prayed. I prayed for those things I wanted, whatever it was at the moment that I thought would fill my needs. When I didn't get what I wanted, the way I wanted it, when I wanted it, I told myself either that I was doing it wrong—that God didn't care about some stupid little nothing person—or that there was no God.

As I got older, I still attempted to pray. But here again, I insisted that God do what I wanted. Yes, I thought I was the director of my life, I knew what was best for me, and I couldn't understand what God's problem was. Maybe he just didn't like me. Maybe he didn't hear me.

In a story I heard years ago, a man was on vacation near the sea. Early one morning, he rose and walked to the cliffs to enjoy the view. As he edged closer, his feet hit loose ground and he slipped over the edge. Halfway down, he grabbed a branch and held on for dear life. He yelled at the top of his lungs, "God, help me!"

A booming voice from the sky said, "Let go of the branch."

The man hesitated, looked into the sky and said, "Is there anyone else up there?"

Like me, he asked for help, but then denied that God knew what was best for him. One must wonder why he bothered to ask.

In my own life I began to wonder too. I never seemed to get what I wanted. And I was convinced if I could just get those things I desired in life, I would be happy.

After all, isn't that what we are all seeking in

life? We strive for happiness, we pray for happiness, we do all manner of things to make ourselves happy. Perhaps the paradox is that we can't make ourselves happy as long as we are striving for it on our own—as long as we think we are the director of our destiny.

We humans spend a great deal of time, energy, money, and thought on how to look better. If we look better, we think, we might feel better about who we are, about our lives. We groom ourselves in the morning, exercise to keep our bodies in shape, eat special diets, choose clothes that flatter, select shoes that make our feet look smaller, buy jewelry that draws attention to whichever part of the body we most want to highlight, and go to places where we can gather with those who are like us. And still there is something missing. So we take medications and drink alcohol to ward off depression, anxiety, even suicidal thoughts. The next day, we start all over again.

But what if, for one day, you got up and changed your routine? Most people can do almost anything for just one day. So what if, this morning, you spent your exercise time exercising your faith instead? What if you spent that time in prayer and meditation instead of aerobics? What if, the next time you want to go shopping for more clothes, shoes, and makeup, you gave the money you would have spent to someone who might not even own one pair of shoes? Instead of clubbing the night away, what if you volunteered your time helping abused animals? What if you went for one day without taking the medications or drinking the alcohol that keeps you from thinking about your life, about the world around you? Sound drastic? Remember, you can do almost anything for just one day.

If you have trouble getting started in prayer,

try placing your shoes under the bed. As you kneel to retrieve them, stay there and say a prayer—not for what you think you want, but to ask what God's will is for you that day. Let go of the branch for just one day, and see what happens.

You might wonder what you should do, where you should be. But when you turn your will over to God, he will put you where you need to be, with the people you need to be with. You won't have to seek out people who need you, or those you need. They will be put in your path. You simply need to recognize the opportunities and act on them. Smile at strangers. Help where you can.

Opening ourselves to God, through prayer, accepting his will for us, doesn't mean you can't be yourself. There's no need to wear a horse-hair shirt and spend your life in constant prayer and meditation. All it means is turning your will over to a God of your choosing on a daily basis, and following his lead. For instance, say you've made plans for the day, perhaps a massage, lunch with a friend. On the way to the restaurant, you see a starving kitten by the side of the road. You have been given an opportunity to make a choice.

The reason that story comes to mind is because it actually happened to me. My husband and I had worked hard all year and were about to embark on a Florida vacation, to escape the cold winter of Illinois. After a long day at work, about a week before we were to leave, my intentions were to go to the mall, shop for vacation clothes, and meet my husband for supper. As I drove past a fast-food restaurant, there it was—a small black kitten, drenched from the sleet, crying on the sidewalk. People were walking around him as if he didn't exist.

I pulled over to the side of the road and

scooped him up. He was so skinny, it was like lifting a feather. He was alone, scared, and hungry, and it made my heart hurt just to look at him. After drying him off, warming him next to my body, I took him to an animal hospital in the next town. I sat for a couple of hours until they could see him, and I spent all my clothes money, and part of our vacation money, on vet bills.

Within days, he was a healthy, happy kitten, running around our house like he owned it. But we already had two dogs, one dog of our own and a stray I'd picked up a few days before the kitten. I couldn't see how we could go on vacation in less than a week. I asked God to show me the way.

Miracles do happen. It was in November, near election time. I'd already gone around our little town, searching for the owners of the dog, asking everyone I knew if they wanted to give a home to the kitten. Two days before our departure, the phone rang. The man said, "I think you may have my dog." He said his wife had been standing in a line waiting to vote, and she asked the clerk if she'd heard of anyone finding an older golden retriever recently. The woman standing in line behind her worked in the grocery store where I shopped. She told her I'd found a dog. You might think that's not so amazing, but the woman lived two towns away from us, and the dog had been missing for nearly a month. They'd had the dog since it was six weeks old and brought it with them from Colorado. It was quite a reunion, a happy day for us all.

The next morning when I went to work, I heard that the guy who ran the bar beneath my shop had to put his old cat to sleep. Apparently, he'd had it for many years and was devastated. Boy, did I have something wonderful for him.

But because he was grieving, I knew he'd say no if I asked him if he wanted another cat. So I called my husband and asked him to bring the kitten to town. Once it was in my arms, I called the bar owner and asked him to come up. I knew as soon as he looked into the kitten's beautiful green eyes, his heart would melt. And it did. The cat lived with him and gave him great joy for many years.

I've heard it said that God laughs while we're making plans, and the kitten experience brought it home to me. It was great that we got to go on our vacation, but it would have been okay if we couldn't. I learned that sometimes we must put our own needs and wants aside and simply do the right thing, and things work out the way they are supposed to. Imagine if I'd passed up that little kitten, or left that poor stray dog in a field to die. How much would I have enjoyed a trip to

Florida carrying those pictures in my mind. God's plans for me were different than my own. Even if I hadn't been able to go on vacation, I wouldn't have traded the looks on those people's faces, the feelings I got as I saw those sick animals come back to health, for all the vacations in the world. There was a sunshine in my heart that no tropical sun could ever bring.

Praying isn't asking for what we want, the way we want it, when we want it. It's about believing that God will lead us and give us what we need, put us where we need to be. It's about being involved in life and taking responsibility for the choices we make every day. For, you see, we are involved in life, in humanity, from the day we are born, and the choices we make today, at this moment, will not only affect us, but others as well.

And isn't it wonderful that every day we get is a new beginning, an opportunity to start over and make a difference. Maybe this is your day to let go of the branch, to slip those shoes under the bed and stay for a while and pray, to turn your will over to God and see what the day brings, what God has planned for you. A myriad of experiences and people are waiting to meet you, but only you can open the door. True happiness could be just across the threshold.

3 *Things Aren't Always What They Seem*

*A*re you one of those people who say, "I've tried prayer and it didn't work." Perhaps a loved one was in an accident and you stayed by their side, prayed night and day, but the loved one still died. Perhaps you'd worked hard for years but were in a bad financial situation, and the job you prayed for went to another; you might say, "Prayer doesn't work." And what if you are born with disabilities? Can you pray those away?

Sometimes, the most tragic events in our lives will lead us to our path. Did you ever notice, when a devastating event takes place, that our world stops? It brings us to a crossroads, our perspective has been drastically altered, and we must make a choice about which way to go. The key word here is *choice.*

Some choose to do something constructive with what they've learned through tragedy. Consider parents, after losing a child to a drunk driver, who have gone on to change laws and make such drivers more accountable. Their accomplishment might not have saved their own child, but only God knows how many other lives have been saved because the new laws encourage designated drivers. Maybe their loss was exactly what they needed to take them on a path to help others, to fulfill their destiny.

Or consider a man who didn't get the promotion he wanted; perhaps he simply wasn't where he needed to be. Being passed over might make him reconsider the path he'd chosen, spur him to walk away, to move away from that seemingly safe job, into the unknown world where his life awaits. We've all heard stories about people who have been forced out, downsized, pressured to retire early, even let go because someone new has taken over. The reason for the crisis doesn't really matter, but the choices made afterward do. In the stories I've heard, those who turned to prayer, who allowed God to lead them, say the "loss" was the best thing that ever happened to them. It was a turning point in their life.

That happened to me. All my life I'd been making costumes for extra money, costumes for children, for every occasion. It was my passion, and it seemed to be a God-given talent. However, I'd never been in the position to earn a living from it, so I always had to work and make costumes on the side.

The day came when I could fulfill my dream. I had the chance to open my own costume shop. It was a wonderful experience. I could barely contain my excitement and was so grateful to God for this opportunity. I prayed every day, I worked hard, sometimes into the wee hours of morning, and I became successful.

As my one-room shop grew to fifteen rooms, as I won many awards, as I was thriving in my business, tragedy struck in the form of Graves' disease, the leading cause of hyperthyroidism. I pushed on, attempted to continue, but the disease had other ideas. I awakened every day exhausted, itched so bad I had to wear my clothing inside out because the seams burned my skin, and watched my hair fall out into the sink. My heart raced, my cholesterol rose dangerously high, and my eyelids retracted. The new medication caused me to have progressive cataracts, and within three months I could barely see. Even after I was diagnosed and treated with radioactive iodine to kill my thyroid, I was looking at years of recovery and eye surgeries.

I didn't understand. I'd been told that when something was right, all the doors would open, and when it wasn't right, no matter what I did, they wouldn't. The doors had opened for me to be a costumer. Why then, my mind screamed, after all those years of hard work, of seeing my dream come to life, would it all be taken away?

The illness brought me down to a point of not being able to run my shop. I was unable to see to make costumes, and I couldn't even take care of my house. In desperation, and probably because I was driving him crazy, my husband reminded me that I'd always wanted to write a book. I thought about it, I prayed about it, and when my husband brought me home an old typewriter, I made the choice. It was something I could do. With no education in the field and little knowledge, I began to write. It was the best thing that ever happened to me.

God may have closed a door for me, but he opened a window. At the crossroads of tragedy, my life began again. I'd always had a desire to write a book, but it was one of those things that I thought would never happen. I did the footwork: wrote the books, mailed them off to publishers, and turned them over to God. If it was right, the doors would open. And they did.

It comes down to this: if you are walking into brick walls, feeling as if you have to tear down buildings to get where you are going, it's probably not where you need to be. If you really want to know where your path leads, all you need is the willingness to ask. It's a simple question: "God, what is your will for me?" You might be amazed at the answer. I certainly never dreamed that I would be an author. Go figure! The way my life had gone, I decided if I were ever able to write my life story, I would call it, "You Can't Get Here from Where I Started—without Divine Intervention." And my divine intervention came through prayer and the acceptance of God's will for me in my life each day.

When we are in the middle of a tragic situation, it's not easy to hold fast to the idea that God wants the best for us, wants to show us the path to the life we were sent here to live out, but it is possible. When things are going well, it's easy to have faith in God, to turn our life over in prayer on a daily basis. The test of faith is when life turns on us, when God asks us to believe it will be okay, that there is a reason and a season for all things.

When we become able to live in the moment, to turn our will and our lives over to a God of our understanding each day, there comes a knowing that things are not always what they seem.

There is a story of two angels. An older angel was sent to Earth with a younger angel, to teach him. As they walked down the road together, the weather turned harsh. They had no money or shelter, so they stopped at the first house they came upon. It was a fine house with many rooms. They knocked at the door and asked to be sheltered for the night.

The owner left them shivering in the rain while he decided whether to allow them in. Finally, he bid them enter through the servants' entrance in the back, so as not to dirty his floors. They were sent to a small basement room to sleep on cots. As they settled in, hungry, chilled to the bone, the older angel noticed a hole in the wall. He searched the basement for plaster and tools, and repaired the hole. The next morning they were sent on their way, without so much as coffee to warm them.

The younger angel was confused as they continued on their journey. He said, "I don't understand. We were treated badly, slept in that terrible basement, were not given any food, yet you fixed the hole in the wall. Why?"

The older angel smiled and said, "Things aren't always what they seem." The night drew near, cold and windblown. Again they sought shelter for the night. It was a small farmhouse. When they knocked, the wife opened the door, saw the two men, and bid them to enter. The poor couple had little but shared with the two angels all they had, and let them sleep in their bed that night. During the night, the farmer's mule died. The mule was the only thing they had to pull the plow that allowed them to survive. Still, in the morning they again shared what little food they had with the angels and wished them well on their journey.

Again the young angel was confused. He said, "I don't understand. These people who had little, gave us all they had, and yet you allowed their mule to die. Why?"

The older angel smiled and said, "Things aren't always what they seem."

At noon, when they came across an apple tree by the road, they sat and ate their fill. Then the young angel said, "What do you mean, things aren't always what they seem?"

The older angel said, "On the first night,

when we slept in the basement, I noticed that behind the wall was a stash of jewels that had been there since the Civil War, so I covered the hole. On the second night at the farmhouse, where the people were so kind, in the night the angel of death came. Instead of allowing him to take the wife, I gave him the mule. Things are not always what they seem."

This story has been with me for some time. It is one that I think of often when I hear of others in crisis or difficult things crop up in my own life. And what it has taught me is to mind my own business and leave God to his. My business is to ask for his will for me, accept it to be for the best, do the footwork, and leave the results to him. Tragedy can be a sheep in wolf's clothing.

4

Taking Care of Unfinished Business

*H*ave you ever had little flashbacks from the past? You might be having a perfectly good day, running here and there, doing this and that, and someone will say something or you'll see something that triggers an old memory you wish you could escape.

I have found that those flashbacks serve a purpose today. They tell us of unfinished business, things we did that are still affecting us, keeping us from the pure joy of living in the moment.

If you are turning your will and life over to God on a daily basis, and these things still keep entering your mind, maybe it's a message to take care of them. Can you clear your mind with prayer? You can ask God to forgive you, but that might not be enough. If the thoughts are still there, the message could be that you need to take action. A better prayer might be for God to give you the opportunity to tell those you have harmed how sorry you are, to make things right.

Since, in many cases, there are other people involved, the hardest part of taking care of unfinished business is staying in your part of it. You see, it doesn't matter what they have done to you because they don't have to face your mirror every morning, live inside your head, deal with whatever flashback is haunting you.

I know, from experience, that until yesterday is resolved, today will carry remorse and guilt like a yoke around my neck, a weight that only I have the power to remove. I believe God can forgive you for any action, but to forgive yourself, you must do what you can to make it right. For me, prayer without action very seldom works. Row yourself into the middle of the lake and try praying yourself back. Until you pick up that oar, you're going nowhere.

Imagine a specific situation from the past that still lives in you today. When you do your morning prayer, when you ask God to help you, you turn your will and life over to him for that day, talk it out, tell him how you feel. It's the cheapest therapy you'll ever get. After you've asked for the opportunity to resolve the past issue, then become willing to recognize it when it shows itself and have the courage to act. When it's over, there will be such a feeling of relief and a joy like you have never known before. You will feel a weight lifted from your shoulders, will truly understand being able to live in the moment, in the day, unfettered by the past.

True happiness on a daily basis comes from

not having any secrets—those things you think you buried deep in your past that no one knows about except you and God, those things you will take to your grave. The point is, you know about them, and you know that God knows. Once you say them out loud, they are no longer a secret and can never come back to hurt you again.

Let's say you've recognized a past problem. You've gone to God in prayer to find a way to resolve it. He's shown you the way and you acted on it. God has forgiven you, and when he forgives, it's like he buries it and it never happened. The other person has forgiven you too. Now comes the hard part. Can you forgive yourself?

In my mind, if you have done your part and asked God to forgive you, but you refuse to forgive yourself, you have set yourself above God. Why must you keep digging up old wounds? A wise man once told me that any time you hold on that hard to something that causes you that much pain, you are getting something out of it. You must decide what the payoff is. Is it an excuse to fail? Is it an excuse to be self-destructive? It's not easy for some of us to let go of those familiar negative feelings, to accept that we can be successful and happy.

Have you ever had one of those days when all was right with the world, that brief moment when you felt totally at peace? Did you cherish that moment, that day when you felt one with God and the world? Imagine being able to hold on to the feeling more often than not. It's possible when you truly turn your will over each day, when you are aware of what needs to be taken care of, you do it, and can honestly forgive yourself as God has forgiven you.

The thing that happens when you learn to resolve past transgressions is it keeps you from a repeat performance, so you never have to go back and do it again. You will have a true understanding of what it is to live in the day, to take care of those problems that arise, when the moment is at hand. Your steps will be lighter, your heart unafraid, your rest deeper, and your mind clearer. You will be blessed with peace and know a new happiness and gratitude with each new sunrise.

5

Living in God's Light

*W*ould it be better to know when we will die? Would we live differently if we did? If we were born knowing the day that our existence on Earth would end, would it make life easier or harder?

We aren't given that knowledge, so who's to say? But if you wander through a cemetery and look at the dates on the tombstones, if you talk to those who have lost loved ones, it becomes obvious that death is blind when it comes to age. Some never make it into this world, and others live more than a hundred years.

Personally, I know the days of my life. I get one day. The beginning of the day is birth and the end of the day is death. There are no tomorrows. I will live each day as if it is a lifetime.

If you believed this would be your last day on this Earth and there was nothing you could do to change it, wouldn't you grasp every minute and make it count? Would all those petty differences, all those things that make you so angry, so unhappy, have any importance in that one day? Wouldn't you attempt to fill that day with wonderful memories, people you love, and surround yourself with love and happiness?

So why dwell in the dream of tomorrow? I've heard all those old sayings. "Tomorrow will be a better day." "Sleep on it, and it will look better tomorrow." Wouldn't it be better to say, "What can you do about it today to make it better?" Then do what you can, and if there is nothing you can do, why waste your day worrying about it?

I've never understood how sleeping on a problem will make it look better the next day. For me, it is better to deal with the problem if I can, turn it over to God if I can't, and then go to sleep. Yes, then it might look better if I get another day. The last thing I want to do if I'm granted another day is enter it with problems.

In the birth of a new day, in my willingness to turn my will and life over to God, I say, Take me, do with me what you will, I trust that you know what is best, and I believe it. So if you believe in God, why worry? And if you worry, why believe in God? After all, what is the point in going to God if you think you know what's better for you?

In your day, in your lifetime, how do you know what your will is and what is God's will? I don't have a definitive answer. But I don't think God's will for us is to live our day hoping tomorrow will be better. It's not to live our day doing harm to others or ourselves and thinking there will be time to fix it later. It's not to dwell in the ego of self, to puff ourselves up like a big blowfish, to set ourselves apart from our fellow human beings. And it's not to say, "I live in God's light" and then be unhappy. That really makes him look bad. Because those who are truly living in the moment, in God's light—not waiting for tomorrow and tomorrow and all the tomorrows they may never get—they will shine today and spread the light in every dark corner they encounter.

There is one thing about living with our minds on the future: it certainly keeps us from focusing on today. A person can still have dreams and goals, but wouldn't it be wonderful if they could enjoy the pursuit of the goal, the daily process they give to something they have a passion for each day? The end result is not ours anyway.

I once knew a man who wanted to build a house. His house would be exactly the way he wanted it. He knew it would take some time to achieve the ultimate goal of his perfect house. And so he began. He hired help. He fired help. He lost his temper on a daily basis because things weren't going as he planned. When he wasn't yelling at the workers, he was thinking about what wasn't right in the building. It put a strain on his family, on his health, on everyone he spent time with. People began to avoid him because all he did was complain about the house. Finally, the house was near completion. He died of a heart attack before he spent the first night in that perfect house. He would have been better off to have lived in a one-room shack. That's not to say he wouldn't have died, but at least he might have lived well until that time.

Through my own life experiences, through watching others, through prayer, I've decided that if you live with one foot in yesterday and one foot in tomorrow, you'll fall flat on your face today. Today: that wonderful moment in time you have been given to do with what you will. It is a gift from God, and you have the choice to throw it away or embrace it. Know that it could be the last gift you get on this Earth.

6

After We Pray

What can we pray for? We can pray for anything we want as long as we understand that sometimes the answer is no. Imagine what life would be like if we got everything we prayed for. I know I would be a mess.

Like the vigilant parent, God knows to keep us from our self-will. If you had a child who wanted to eat nothing but ice cream, would you allow it? If you did, and this overweight, unhealthy child turned eighteen, would you then send him out into the world as an adult and say, "Go and eat vegetables"?

Such is life. It takes many life lessons to ready

us for the time when we go out into the world and share ourselves with others. For some of us, the journey to spiritual maturity takes longer. For whatever reasons, we fall into bad habits, become indifferent to life, embrace fears, become cynical, and miss opportunities to grow and change. As they say, insanity is doing the same self-destructive behavior over and over and expecting different results.

It's like taking a test in school. If they keep giving us the same test, and we fail to prepare for it, to do well, we will be taking it over many times. At least with God, there is the chance to try again, to redeem ourselves, as long as there is breath in our bodies.

I always wonder if there is such a thing as reincarnation. Let's say there is. Do I want to come back and do this all over again? I think not. I've decided to give it my best shot this time around.

And even if we don't have to come back, what if the things we don't learn here, the things that aren't resolved, still have to be resolved on the other side? Not a pleasant thought.

So, as we move through this life, when things happen that are out of our control, when seemingly tragic events take place, how we deal with them, what we learn from them, what we do afterward, is important.

I met and got to know a nice woman many years ago. Her life experiences had been totally different from mine. She'd been raised in a good, loving home, with an abundance of things, with Christian ethics and values. She grew up well, married a man who would continue the life that she'd known, and worked for the church they were involved in. They produced healthy children. It seemed like the perfect life.

One day, as we had coffee in her nice house,

she said to me, "I wish I believed in God the way you do."

I was stunned. My life had been the complete opposite of hers; the struggle to survive, to find a God in my life, had been long and painful. I was a late bloomer.

"I think of God on Sundays and Wednesdays," she continued, "When I am in church."

Not so for me. My very survival and any peace and happiness I've had was dependent on turning my will and life over to God on a daily basis.

As our conversation continued, I began to understand. I had always believed that those who lived like this woman were the lucky ones, the chosen ones, whose life hadn't been filled with pain and anguish. Yet in all her life, her faith had never been challenged; she'd not been given the opportunities I'd had to walk through the pain, the fear, the uncertainty.

Several years later, she contracted a deathly illness. As we spoke, just before she died, I could hear the anger and resentment she felt toward God. She believed she'd done everything right, moved through life doing what was expected of her. Why was God punishing her like this?

Her life, what happened to her, gave me pause to reflect, to look at my own life, to understand that God can't live just in our heads but must live in all that we are. It's easy to say, "Yes, I think there's a God. I pray on Sundays. I give to the church." But knowing that feeling in the deepest core of our beings, knowing that God is in our lives every day, every moment, is as essential for our well-beings as the air we breathe. To me that is faith.

I never expect that things won't happen in my life. In fact, I expect that they will. I remember crying to a friend of mine once—you know, the old, "Why me?" thing.

He said, "Why not you? What makes you think you are any better than I am—or anyone else?"

I'd never quite looked at it that way, but that's what happens. When we have questions in our mind, when we become spiritual seekers, the answers are given to us, but we must be willing to hear them.

So how do we move God from our heads to our hearts? We begin by questioning what we believe, what our truth is, where our life has led us. If we have a great deal of material things but always feel as if something is missing, or if we have little and are unhappy in our life even when things are going well, it's time to take a hard look at the choices we've made and are continuing to make.

I know it's difficult to believe that, no matter your circumstances, you have a choice to be happy or unhappy on any given day. It's all in your perspective. If what you've been doing isn't working, if you face life on a daily basis in quiet desperation or in rage, if you knew there was another person who could give you a way out of your dilemma, wouldn't you go to them for answers? There is someone. Why not ask?

In the beginning, you don't even have to truly believe or be totally convinced; you simply have to make the effort. Open your mind, bend your knees, ask for help, stay out of the way, and watch God do his stuff.

That's exactly what happened to me many years ago. I lived in a small town in Illinois. Because of my actions, I wasn't exactly well thought of. I got down on my luck, was barely surviving. I needed a job but couldn't find anyone who would take a chance on me. Someone had suggested that I pray.

Not me. I hung in there, begged for jobs, continued to walk into walls, and when I was about at the end of my rope, I did what he suggested. Oh, I didn't get down on my knees; I wasn't even particularly humble. But I said, "Okay, God, you put a job in front of me, and I'll take it." I don't even think I signed off with an "Amen."

The following day, I went to the local coffee shop. I hung out there in hopes of making a connection for a job. I sat down with a man I knew. Shortly after that, another man entered. I didn't know him, but he was acquainted with the man across from me. My friend asked him to join us; then he asked me if I'd found a job. I said I hadn't. The stranger said, "Are you looking for work? I know a woman who is looking for someone to look after her mother."

Not exactly the type of work I had in mind, but the groceries were about gone and soon I would be on the street.

He handed me a phone number. I called from the coffee shop because I didn't have a phone. The woman's daughter said they had help, but she would keep my number in case it didn't work out. I figured it was another dead end. But two days later, in the same coffee shop, there was a message for me to get in touch with the woman. The hair stood up on the back of my neck, my heart beat a little faster as my prayer replayed itself in my mind. Could this really work?

I was given the opportunity to care for one of the finest women I'd ever known, until she passed away. As she lay in her bed, crippled with Parkinson's disease and other problems, and although I was being paid to care for her, she was the one who helped me. She didn't whine or complain, had an enduring belief in God, taught me about dignity and self-respect, but most of all about faith. Yes, God put me exactly where I needed to be. God heard that unholy little prayer and decided maybe, just maybe, this time I would let him lead the way.

What had I done differently this time? I'd attempted to pray before. But when I prayed, I told God exactly what I wanted him to do. No sense leaving things to chance, out of my control. And, of course, nothing happened.

But this time it was different. Whether I'd realized it at the time or not, I'd turned my life over to him, if only in that one thing: a job. It was a start. He didn't put me where I would have—it certainly wasn't the type of work I would have sought out—but what I got out of it was more than money could buy.

The messages, the life lessons, the answers to our prayers come in many forms. They can come through total strangers, friends, even those you consider enemies, in the strangest ways and places. But if we don't seek, they won't come; if we don't listen, we won't hear them; and if we don't open ourselves to the possibilities, we won't find the path that will lead to a better way of life.

Perhaps the next time you're stuck, not sure which way to turn, you might try turning that one thing over for one day and see what happens. Be aware that God works in mysterious ways, so you have to pay attention. When you open yourself up to the possibilities and let God take the lead, all things are possible.

7

Prayer Is Talking, Meditation Is Listening

*W*hen you think of meditation, what comes to mind? Do you see yourself sitting for hours on a rug, legs folded over each other, the scent of perfumed candles filling the air? Don't laugh. That's what I pictured the first time someone suggested that I try meditation.

What I found to be true, for me, was that meditation is nothing more than a self-imposed time-out—yes, like sending a child to his room or to a quiet corner alone, to think about what he's done.

Life is full of problems and choices, but it is also full of noise. Consider all the machines we have in our homes that make noise. Most of us have at least one television, a telephone, a computer, computer games, and any number of appliances that emit sounds. Outside, automobiles buzz around, horns blare, sirens whine, and people talk.

These myriad noises have become such an accepted part of life, many people can't go to sleep without them. To help them sleep, there are recordings of the rain forest, sounds of the jungle, the rustling of a babbling brook. Some people leave their television or radio on just for the noise. But think about it: if we are surrounded by noise, from whatever source, we don't have to listen to what's going on in our mind. And what if that's where the answers to life's problems are?

We pray. We ask for answers, and then we don't listen. Meditation is nothing more than a quiet time after the prayer, to wait for an answer. The answer won't be faxed, telephoned in, televised, or digitized. It will come through that small voice from within. Some call it instincts, others say it is conscience, but I call it my God voice. It's that part of me that knows everything about me, the truth of my existence, my past experiences, my desires, resentments, secret dreams—and, somewhere deep inside, the solution to whatever problem is haunting me.

When I think of meditation, it reminds me of going to the doctor. We get undressed, sit naked and alone on the table until the doctor arrives. As she examines us, we list the symptoms we have. When that is finished, would we just stand up and walk out? Of course not; we would give her the time to tell us what she thinks. Otherwise, why bother going in the first place?

With meditation, I don't think it matters what

position you sit in, where you sit, or how long you sit; the answer comes when it will. One reason there are books explaining how to meditate is because sometimes we have to put our bodies in a certain position to understand why we are there. It's similar to prayer: we don't have to be kneeling in a church to pray; it's one tool we can carry with us wherever we go. It's the same with meditation. We could be standing on a mountaintop, sitting by an open fire, lying in a pool. We can use it wherever and however we wish.

But if you are one of those people who needs to commit to a physical ritual to reinforce the purpose of what you're doing, that's all right too. You can buy a rug, teach yourself the lotus position, purchase candles and a book that tells you to sit quietly, with no distractions, and imagine roots from the earth twining around your body, or to stare into a candle flame so long that when you close your eyes, you can still see it. Or you can simply sit quietly after the prayer and listen.

However you decide to meditate, the answers can come in many forms. They might reveal themselves to you in your true feelings about a situation or another person. They could come through a voice from your life, someone who gave you a truth many years ago—a parent, teacher, coach, religious mentor, yes, even that homeless man you spoke to on the street. They could come from a book you read yesterday, or last year; there is often a reason a particular passage comes to mind.

I believe God reveals the answers to us in a frame of reference that we can understand. For instance, when I had to decide whether to take another chance at a relationship with someone I'd known before, and I didn't know what to do,

I turned to prayer and then meditation. As I sat quietly listening to the thoughts that passed through my mind, one thought repeated itself over and over: "What was, was; and what is, is." That saying had been a favorite of someone in my past, someone I respected and admired. It wasn't exactly what I thought a message from God would be like, but it worked for me at that moment. I pursued the relationship, and my life has been greatly enhanced through it. This person has been my husband and best friend for nearly eighteen years. There would be a great empty spot in my life today if I hadn't taken the time to listen after the prayer.

Each person we meet, every situation we've encountered in our lives, has brought us to this point, and I believe there are reasons for all of them. To look at the positive side of our lives, each circumstance out of the past is like an insurance policy. It's there when we need it—that ability to survive through crisis, that person who gave us something we might not need for years but is stored within. God can use it to guide us, if we listen.

What is the truth that comes from such belief? That I cannot live against myself, live in a state of compromise, and expect to be happy. When we go to God in prayer, when we truly listen for the answer, recognize it, and then talk ourselves out of it—or allow others to talk us out of it— that is living against what we know is right for us. It's between us and God, the only ones who know the totality of who we are, warts and all, and love us anyway.

If you are not all that fond of yourself, know that once you believe in a God, develop a relationship with him, you will understand that you are a product of something wonderful, even if it's not perfect. How can you believe otherwise? God doesn't make trash.

So after your next prayer, stay for a while and listen. Listen to the small voice within, that God voice that will lead you where you need to be in life. The answers are not always the easy ones, but they are the best ones. The answers might require us to do difficult things, or take risks we have been reluctant to take, but a life well lived, and an afterlife filled with happiness, will be our reward.

Each of us must find our own comfort zone with meditation, just as in prayer. There are books to read, tapes to listen to, and many different methods. But meditation is nothing more than a time-out—a time away from noise, the pressures of the day, too much information, family problems, the hustle and bustle of everyday survival. I see it as a miniretreat, where my mind can take me wherever I need to be that day. I can imagine a serene beach near the ocean, the waves rolling in and out with the beat of my heart, or I can sit atop a mountain, the peaks covered by the snow, and not feel the cold. I can watch an eagle ride the air currents and smile at the beauty of the experience. I am only limited by my imagination. And in my meditative state, I become a part of all I see. The more I feel a part of all I see, the more connected I feel to the earth around me, to those who live on it, and the God I've come to believe in.

The ultimate answer to life and happiness, for me, is an understanding of who I am, what I am a part of, and the acceptance of where life takes me on any given day. I've finally figured out that it's all good if you listen and learn. Meditation is just another tool. Most likely, it will not bring you fame and riches, but if you acquire them, it will teach you the best way to use them. It might not bring you the love of your life, but if you do connect with that person, it will have taught you how to listen, which will enhance your relationship. But the best thing it will teach you is who you are, what you are willing to accept, what you are not willing to accept in life, and how to live in the solution instead of in the problem.

Why not try it for just one day? What will it cost you but a little time and a few words? Go to the God of your choosing, ask for help and guidance, then take the time to be still and listen. If it doesn't work, life will refund your misery. You have nothing to lose and everything to gain.

8

To Believe or Not to Believe

There are many ideas about why we are here, about whether there is a purpose or whether a couple of heavenly bodies simply bumped together accidentally. I've read and listened to others' ideas on the subject, and I've come to the conclusion that it doesn't matter. We're here. Deal with it.

There are those who have avoided living life, who are in a state of "analysis paralysis." Nothing will hold you back more than searching for answers to questions that can't be answered. I'm not just speaking of those who are attempting to find answers to the beginning of time, but those who question everything and if they don't hear, see, and touch the answer, they continue searching, waiting for proof.

Imagine for a moment that through some situation, you lost all your identification, and the computers were down. How would you prove who you are? A name is just a name unless you have a driver's license, credit card, birth certificate, something that says this is me, John Doe. You could talk all day, but you won't be cashing any checks.

Yet we ask this of God. Prove to me you are there. If I pray for something and don't get it, does that mean God doesn't exist? If I ask for a sign, and don't see it, is there a God? Can you think of anything more ridiculous? Do you think God is going to stand in front of us and hand out a business card that says, "God. Humanity is my business, Eternity is my game. Call 1-800-Prayer"? Even then, would we believe?

Ultimately, every human being has a choice in what they believe. For instance, for those of you who believe the Big Bang theory, what if God caused those heavenly bodies to bump together? Prove that he didn't.

When it comes to spirituality, to God, to prayer, there will always be questions for which there are no answers, at least in this lifetime. The proof of life, of God, of how prayer works is through personal experience.

If you're agnostic—if you say, "I just don't know,"—and the day comes that you find yourself in a precarious situation, with no other human being around to help you, would you change your mind and pray for help? Most of us would and do. If you did and things went well, would you then say there is a God and prayer does work? Or, if you continued in the situation for hours or days, until someone came along who might save you but doesn't and you ended up disabled, would you say there is no God and prayer doesn't work? If the person who came along *did* save you and then became the love of your life, would you then say there is a God and prayer does work? It's the old chicken-and-egg thing.

Instead of waiting until we are in the bottom of a pit, in a turned-over car, or caught in a flood, wouldn't it be better to choose now to believe, to experiment with prayer? What is it we are waiting for, a disaster?

I'm as guilty as anyone. Before I came to prayer, I dug myself into a hole so deep, so dark, I didn't think there was any way out. My best efforts had me sitting at the bottom of the hole. I was so confused. I didn't really believe—didn't have that knowing feeling—but there had to be a better way, a reason for my existence, something good about my life, something I could do to make it better. I'd met a woman who I admired, who I saw as a happy, content individual. There was something in her eyes, in her manner that drew me to her. I wanted what she had. I sought her out. I told her my problem.

She said, "Try getting up in the morning and reading three spiritual things out loud. You don't have to make them up, find already-written prayers. You don't have to agree with them, understand them, or believe them; just be willing to do it."

It sounded crazy, but I was desperate. I searched through books and magazines, found three prayers, cut them out and taped them to the bathroom mirror. The first morning, I felt awkward standing in the bathroom, alone, reading someone else's prayers, but I did it. Not much changed that day other than that the words from those prayers stayed with me, flitted in and out my mind as the day went by. The next morning, I did it again—and the next morning, and the next.

In a short time, something happened. My circumstances hadn't changed. I still lived in half of a garage, my old car still didn't run most of the time, so I still had to walk to work, there was no more money than ever, but something was different. My steps were lighter as I walked to work, my mind clearer. I hummed, I smiled at people on the street, and for the first time in years, there was a flicker of hope in my heart. It seemed that I'd forgotten to dread the day.

A funny thing happened on my way to God. I began with the words of others, finally found my own, and eventually came to believe.

I found the answer to those age-old questions, Is there a God? Does prayer work? Yes, there is in my life, and prayer is the connection.

I consider myself a walking miracle. And the only thing I did differently was pray. Today, every day is a gift, and what I do with that gift is up to me. Today, I get to be exactly who I am. Today, I don't owe anybody anything anymore. Whatever I give is with an open hand and an open heart. Today, I hope to be like that woman I went to for answers, that woman who shared her experience, strength, and hope with me so freely. Today, all I have to do is pray for the day, and let God put me where I'm supposed to be, with the people I need to be with—and keep my mind open to what he wants me to do. And, if today my life should end, I'll feel I've been overpaid.

In the farthest reaches of my imagination, I could never have dreamed of what God had in store for me, for the life that was waiting for me to surrender. And it all began with the willingness to experiment with prayer, to consider the existence of God. I'm so thankful I stuck around long enough to find it.

However you come to the point in life where you want more, need to make changes in your life, put your preconceived ideas aside, let go of the questions, and find the willingness to try prayer. You might be amazed at the life God has waiting for you. You too could be a miracle waiting to happen.

9 *Making the Connection*

*O*ld habits die hard. The most successful way to overcome an old habit is to
replace it with a new one. To do that, at
least in the beginning, we must make a conscious
effort each day.

We humans are odd creatures. We often hold
on to those old habits with the last breath in our
body, for fear of change, fear of the unknown.
When we stay where we are, doing the same
things, we know what to expect, are comfortable with the familiar, even if it's keeping us
from happiness and peace.

But life is change, whether we like it or not,
and we can either make the decision to stay in an

unhappy existence or experiment with a new way.

If we are overweight and it's causing us anguish, we search out diet and exercise programs. If we are addicted to something, a treatment facility, being with groups of others who have walked through the pain, can help. If we have a physical problem, we seek doctors and medication. Mental problems can be taken care of by specialists in the field. But what of the spiritual? There are no X rays we can take, no blood test, written test, or CAT scan that can pinpoint the problem. The truth lives within us.

If spiritual bankruptcy were listed in a medical journal, it would be called a "symptomatic disease," and the symptoms would be listed as follows:

1. A feeling of not being connected, not fitting in
2. Anxiety about the future

3. Believing we are not worthy
4. Anger, even feelings of rage
5. Fear of new people and situations
6. An inability to trust
7. Feelings of dread and unhappiness
8. Restlessness
9. A general feeling of an unfulfilled life
10. A desperate searching for something outside ourselves to make us feel better

I'm no doctor, but I have suffered through all the symptoms of spiritual bankruptcy. What if I told you there are some simple things you could do to cure the disease? After all, if you went to a doctor with a physical problem that was causing you pain, and he told you there were a few simple exercises you could do to help, wouldn't you try them?

If you have one problem, something that has

been driving you crazy, and you've tried everything to fix it, to no avail—just for one day, and in that one situation, try turning it over to God. The catch is that you have to stop worrying about it. If you continue to hold it in your mind, to try to figure out a solution, you haven't turned it over.

One way I learned to do that is to make a "God Box." It can be any container with a lid on it. Write the word "God" on it. Now write your problem on a piece of paper and slip it inside. Sometimes a physical act helps us to turn it over to God and leave it there. If you start stewing over the problem, take the slip of paper out. When you are ready, put it back in. The hard part of using a God Box is giving up control, knowing the results are not up to us. But if your solutions aren't working, why not give someone else a shot?

If you're having a problem connecting with a

God of your choosing, try the three-word prayer, "God, help me." It won't cost you much, just a few seconds in the morning. Still don't feel connected? Are you one of those people who needs to perform a physical act to make it more real? Try the shoe exercise. Before you go to bed, push your shoes way under the bed—so far under that when you wake, you must get on your knees to retrieve them. While you're there, have a little chat with God.

You say you don't want to get on your knees, and you're having trouble figuring out what to say in prayer? Cut out a couple of prayers or spiritual things and paste them on your mirror. Read them out loud in the morning. Do it until it becomes a habit. Sometimes we just need to bring the body, and the mind will follow.

Whatever words you use in the morning to make your connection, take them with you throughout the day. If you're able to do that, pay attention to how you're feeling. Is the anger starting to slip away? Do the fears seem smaller? Are you experiencing a small glimmer of hope? The more you exercise your spiritual muscle, the stronger it will become. Then you will be ready for more strenuous exercises. Once you become comfortable with daily prayer, you might try sitting quietly for a few minutes afterward, to listen. Will you hear a voice? Not in the way that you would normally think of it. Don't force it, don't try to make it happen. Simply accept the thoughts that come to your mind. You might be surprised at the answers that will come to you in this way. But remember, if you're praying for the truth of a situation, and the truth is revealed, it's time to accept it. You cannot make an informed decision until you know the truth.

One big question that plagued me early on

was, How do I know the difference between my will for me and God's will for me? There are ways to tell. You know those old sayings about snakes: "Black on red, go ahead. Red on black, better get back." Well, I have one for decision making: "If you have a doubt, better back out." If you are turning your will over to God on a daily basis and you're faced with a choice, and you experience reluctance through a niggling little fear in the back of your mind, that is called an instinct for danger. Whatever the niggling little fear was about, it's probably not right for you.

When you get those boulders rumbling around in your belly, it's the same message. Whatever the situation is, no matter how good someone else might make it sound, it's obviously not right for you at that moment. But if you're waiting for a burning bush or loud voice from the sky, you're in for a long wait.

On the other hand, there will be people put in your path to act as guides in certain areas of your life. For instance, let's say you need some extra money to take care of an unexpected expense. You turn it over to God. That day you walk into the grocery store and see a sign, someone is looking for someone to babysit their dog. It will be just enough money to take care of the problem. Accident? I think not.

And this works in all of our affairs. If you are seeking a soul mate—that person to love and to love you—put away that list of what they should look like and act like, and know that God is a great matchmaker. You may not recognize the face, but if you are open to God's will, you will recognize the soul. It will be the person who will love you just as you are. There will be a kind of comfort that makes you feel as if you have known this person all your life, can't imagine a day without your soul mate in it. He or she will never expect more than you are willing to give and won't try to change you. I know this to be true through personal experience.

The only thing we can change in life is ourselves. Just as we are on our path, other people are on theirs, doing what they need to do. Acceptance and compassion is the ability to separate the person from the action. We can like someone and not like what they are doing. So, today, if you are spending time with someone you care about, listening to their problem and their choice for a solution, keep in mind that people will ultimately do what they want no matter what you say. Your job is to plant the seed of truth, but it must grow in God's time. Unless you have lived in their shoes, or have appointed yourself God's little helper, stay in your own business and leave God to his. You won't believe how much stress and anxiety there is in attempting to run the universe—even a small part of it.

Another exercise you might try is smiling and speaking to strangers. You don't have to stop and have a lengthy conversation; simply acknowledge that they exist. It is a terrible thing to feel invisible, but some do. What if that smile, that kind word, that small acknowledgment made a difference in one person's life for that one day? Wouldn't it be worth the effort?

As we try to change old habits, change our lives for the better, it isn't that we will cure all the ills in the world or save the human race, just our little corner of it, the man in the mirror. We can't be of any use to any other human being until we are of use to ourselves.

When you lay your head on the pillow tonight, think of three things you are grateful for and give thanks. It's not that hard. If another person helped you with something, you wouldn't hesitate to say, "Thank you." Even if all you have to be thankful for is enough to eat, a decent place to rest, and your health, that's more than some have. And tell yourself that each morning is a beginning, another day given you through the grace of God. Get excited about life, the adventures that await.

It's only when we surrender our life to a God of our understanding that we find the path to our true life, to the purpose of our being. He's waiting for you to open the door. The key is prayer. The answer is living in the moment, doing the best we can on a daily basis and never comparing ourselves to anyone else.

When life is going well, don't wait for the other shoe to drop, because if you do, it certainly will. Accept what God has to give you with a grateful heart and enjoy it to the fullest. I believe God wants us to have everything wonderful in life; he just doesn't want us to forget where and how we got it.

You will find that when you make a real connection with God on a daily basis, turn your will and life over to God, and live accordingly, the payoff is peace and happiness, and a feeling of freedom understood only by those who have been imprisoned, if only in their hearts and minds. It is the one cure for spiritual bankruptcy, but you must take the treatment every day.

A stranger once said to me, "Someone ought to pay you to walk around and smile." It was the greatest compliment I've ever had. For today, the smile on my face starts deep within my soul. I am truly one of the happiest people I know. Since the day I had my spiritual awakening, gave myself that shot of God every day, I've held on

to that special feeling. No matter what happens,
it will be okay, and I never have to be alone again.
And neither do you.

just
try
this

Afterword

When the opportunity was put in front of me, I chose a God of my understanding to be my guide. Each day, I get up and show up, and ask for his guidance on this unknown journey. I can't wait to see what the new day brings my way. There is no good or bad in my life, simply one experience after another, which will ultimately take me where I need to be. Sometimes, the excitement I feel for life is almost more than I can stand.

And it's so simple. I pray for today and follow that path well worn by one who has gone before. Each day is a world of its own, and I live it to the best of my ability, savoring the moments, knowing the journey could end at any time. Today I stand in awe of my life on a daily basis. God has taken me to places and people that I never could have imagined. And all those things that happened before, those things that seemed so awful, have brought me to a point of being able to help others.

I'd like to share a story with you as an example of what God has done for me. Some years ago, I decided to attend a big writers conference in Maui. I would be going by myself to a place I'd never been, and there would be many famous authors, people from big publishing houses, and the idea made me nervous, to say the least.

At first, I didn't feel like I fit in—those old feelings of poor self-esteem reared their ugly heads. I had to do something, or it was going to be a miserable trip for me. But I also knew:

When in doubt, pray it out. I prayed for guidance and strength.

Later that day, as I walked near the beach, I met a woman. We got to talking about our lives. She asked me if I would be willing to talk to a group of people that evening. I agreed. She picked me up that night and I gave an inspirational talk to a roomful of people.

After I spoke, a younger man approached, obviously emotionally distraught. With tears in his eyes, he hugged me hard and said in my ear, "God sent you here to talk to me." I'm still not completely sure what I said to help him, but one thing I was sure of was that I wasn't in Maui for the writers conference. I truly believe God put me there to talk to that one man. The writers conference was just his excuse to get me there. Once I knew what I was there for, I relaxed and enjoyed my trip to the fullest.

Over and over in my life, God has worked that way. Every day has become an opportunity to live life to the fullest, to understand that there are no accidents, and that God has a plan for me. I think one of the most profound things I can tell you is that I look forward to every day I get, to every moment I have, to every person I meet, to every new experience that comes my way. That's saying a lot for someone who came from where I did. And if there was hope for me, there is for anyone who is simply willing to try, to utter those three little words, "God, help me!"

A Few Simple Prayers

On the following pages are a few of the prayers
I use on a daily basis. If they are helpful to you,
please use them as your own.

Morning Prayer

Early morning is my special time. I love the absolute quiet before the world comes to life. Of one thing I am absolutely certain: when I say my morning prayer, give myself that quiet time, life flows more smoothly and the day always goes much better.

Dear Father,

Thank you for another day.

Be with me this day. Show me the way.

Touch my body, my mind,

and my soul that I might be whole.

Guide me in all that I say, think, and do.

Put me where I need to be,

with the people I need to be with.

Fill me with your love and kindness,

that I may know the way.

Help me to understand your will in all things this day.

Amen

Evening Prayer

When I think of the evening prayer, I think of gratitude. I try never to take people and things for granted because I know how quickly they can all slip away. If I retire for the night after having lived my last day, I don't wish to leave this world with anger and resentments.

Dear Father,
Thank you for this day.
Thank you for all you've given me,
for giving me another chance.
Help my body to rest,
*   to gain strength for the day to come,*
that I might be a blessing in all that I say and do.
Help me to live in your truth.
Amen

A Prayer for Others

We can no more see down the road for another person than we can for ourselves. Whatever they are going through at the moment may be as necessary to their life path as all we've endured has been necessary to ours. Therefore, attempting to save others from their experiences, whatever they may be, is not always a good thing. I try to keep this in mind when I pray for someone else.

Dear Father,
Please be with [name] today.
Guide her and show her the way.
Help her to see the truth,
and give her the strength and willingness to act on it.
Help her to know she is not alone.
Amen

A Prayer for Any Time

When I am confronted with a situation that might be perceived as "bad," I tell myself it's not about "good" or "bad," but simply one life experience after another, leading me to the end of my journey here. This is my prayer for these times.

God,
Help me!

Barb Rogers learned most of her life lessons through great pain and tragedy. After surviving abuse, the death of her children, addiction, and a life-threatening illness, she won her struggle to find a new way of life. She first became a professional costume designer and founded Broadway Bazaar Costumes. When her illness forced her to give up costume designing, Barb became an author, writing two costuming books and creating *Mystic Glyphs: An Oracle Based on Native American Symbols*. She now lives in Arizona with her husband and two dogs.

To Our Readers

Red Wheel, an imprint of Red Wheel/Weiser, publishes books on topics ranging from spunky self-help, spirituality, personal growth, and relationships to women's issues and social issues. Our mission is to publish quality books that will make a difference in people's lives—how we feel about ourselves and how we relate to one another and to the world at large. We value integrity, compassion, and receptivity, both in the books we publish and in the way we do business.

Our readers are our most important resource, and we value your input, suggestions, and ideas about what you would like to see published. Please feel free to contact us, to request our latest book catalog, or to be added to our mailing list.

Red Wheel/Weiser, LLC

P.O. Box 612

York Beach, ME 03910-0612

www.redwheelweiser.com